AFTER JESUS DIED

**The spiritual condition of the disciples
after Jesus died
until the day of Pentecost**

John David Clark, Sr.

After Jesus Died
*The spiritual condition of the disciples after Jesus died
until the day of Pentecost*
© 2018 John David Clark, Sr.

ISBN-978-1-934782-27-9

Cover design by Donna Nelson

Author's Notes

- In English, there is no difference in the singular and plural forms of "you". However, in biblical Hebrew and Greek, the difference is obvious. To more accurately convey the biblical writers' messages in verses where the word "you" appears, I have italicized the "y" of all plural forms, such as *y*ou, *y*our, *y*ours, *y*ourselves.

- Translations of Old and New Testament scriptures are my own. Following standard practice, when a word is added to the translation for clarification, it is italicized.

- Punctuation appears inside quotation marks only when that punctuation is part of what is quoted. To include all periods and commas within quotation marks, as many grammarians demand, leaves too much room, in my opinion, for misrepresentation of the quoted material.

Visit us on the web!
PastorJohnsHouse.com
GoingtoJesus.com

BOOKS OF THE BIBLE AND THEIR ABBREVIATIONS

Old Testament Books

Genesis	Gen.	Ecclesiastes	Eccl.
Exodus	Ex.	Song of Solomon	Song
Leviticus	Lev.	Isaiah	Isa.
Numbers	Num.	Jeremiah	Jer.
Deuteronomy	Dt.	Lamentations	Lam.
Joshua	Josh.	Ezekiel	Ezek.
Judges	Judg.	Daniel	Dan.
Ruth	Ruth	Hosea	Hos.
1Samuel	1Sam.	Joel	Joel
2Samuel	2Sam.	Amos	Amos
1Kings	1Kgs.	Obadiah	Obad.
2Kings	2Kgs.	Jonah	Jon.
1Chronicles	1Chron.	Micah	Mic.
2Chronicles	2Chron.	Nahum	Nah.
Ezra	Ezra	Habakkuk	Hab.
Nehemiah	Neh.	Zephaniah	Zeph.
Esther	Esth.	Haggai	Hag.
Job	Job	Zechariah	Zech.
Psalms	Ps.	Malachi	Mal.
Proverbs	Prov.		

New Testament Books

Matthew	Mt.	1Timothy	1Tim.
Mark	Mk.	2Timothy	2Tim.
Luke	Lk.	Titus	Tit.
John	Jn.	Philemon	Phlm.
Acts	Acts	Hebrews	Heb.
Romans	Rom.	James	Jas.
1Corinthians	1Cor.	1Peter	1Pet.
2Corinthians	2Cor.	2Peter	2Pet.
Galatians	Gal.	1John	1Jn.
Ephesians	Eph.	2John	2Jn.
Philippians	Phip.	3John	3Jn.
Colossians	Col.	Jude	Jude
1Thessalonians	1Thess.	Revelation	Rev.
2Thessalonians	2Thess.		

Contents

Preface

Over the years, I have asked a number of people, "When were the disciples born again?" Every believer should know the answer to that question, for nothing is more fundamental to the gospel than what Jesus called the new birth. However, I have yet to ask that question to anyone who had previously considered it, including ministers. The response I received from one minister represents, in general, the response from them all. He replied, contemplatively, "I've never even thought about it." In the mid-1970s, just one of my seminary professors, in only one class, brought up the subject, but it was almost in passing that he told us there was disagreement among theologians concerning when the disciples were converted (that is, born again).

Some theories concerning when the disciples were born again include the moment Jesus called them to follow him (Mt. 4:18–22); when they were baptized in water in Jesus' name;[1] when Jesus anointed them and sent them out to preach (Mt. 10:1–5); when they partook of the Last Supper meal (Mt. 26:20f); and when the resurrected Jesus breathed on them and said "receive the Spirit" (Jn. 20:21). And there are a few who can give the right answer, which is that the disciples were born again on the day of Pentecost when they were baptized with the holy Spirit and "began to speak in other tongues as the Spirit moved them to speak" (Acts 2:4).

If anyone on earth was born again after Jesus died, and before Pentecost, surely his disciples were – but they were not. If anyone on earth understood his purpose and doctrine after Jesus died, and before Pentecost, surely his disciples did – but they did not. I am certain that the Reader will agree, after reading this little book, that the Bible leaves no reasonable alternative to those two conclusions.

---

[1]The water baptism of none of Jesus' disciples is recorded in the Bible.

AFTER JESUS DIED

**The spiritual condition of the disciples
after Jesus died
until the day of Pentecost**

John David Clark, Sr.

The text is marked in different colors to distinguish God's part in the story from the part of Jesus' followers.

The works and words of God and of Christ are in RED.
The works and words of Jesus' followers are in BLUE.
All other text is in BLACK.

After Jesus Died in Matthew

Matthew 27

50. Then Jesus, again crying out with a loud voice, let go the spirit.

51. And, behold, the veil of the temple was torn in two, from top to bottom, and the earth shook, and the rocks were split apart,

52. and the tombs were opened, and many bodies of saints who had fallen asleep were raised,

53. and after his resurrection, they came out of the tombs and entered into the holy city, and they were seen by many.

54. Now, the captain and those who were guarding Jesus with him, seeing the earthquake and the *other* things that happened, were very frightened and said, "This really was a god's son!"

55. And there were many women there, looking on from a distance, who followed Jesus from Galilee and ministered to him,

56. among whom was Mary the Magdalene, and Mary the mother of James and Joses, and the mother of Zebedee's sons.

Question: Why were these women, righteous and good as they were, just "looking on from a distance," and not rejoicing that the debt for the whole world's sin was being paid and that man's redemption from bondage to his fallen, corrupt nature was at hand?

Answer: They were not aware that the debt for man's sin was being paid or that man even needed to be redeemed from a fallen nature.

¶57. Now, when evening was come, a rich man named Joseph from Arimathea came, who also himself was a disciple of Jesus.

58a. This man approached Pilate and asked for Jesus' body.

Note: Joseph was probably ashamed of himself for fearing to confess his faith in Jesus while Jesus was alive (Jn. 19:38) and was now trying to make up for it by honoring Jesus publicly.

58b. Pilate then commanded that the body be given him.

59. And when he had taken the body, Joseph wrapped it up in a clean linen cloth

60. and laid it in his new sepulcher that he had hewn in a rock, and after rolling a great stone to the entrance of the sepulcher, he went away.

Note: Joseph would have done the same for anyone he loved. This manner of burial was not unusual among well-to-do Jews of the time; it does not suggest that Joseph was born again, or even that he possessed exceptional faith or knowledge of God. On the contrary, Joseph did not believe that Jesus would rise from the dead; otherwise, he would not have shrouded Jesus' body in burial linen.

61. And Mary the Magdalene and the other Mary were there, and they sat down opposite the tomb.

Note: Nothing in this verse indicates that these women were born again and believed that Jesus would rise from the dead. All that we are told here is that they attended Jesus' burial, which they would have done for anyone they loved.

¶62. The next day, that is, after the Preparation, the high priests and the Pharisees gathered before Pilate,

63. saying, "Sir, we remember that while he was alive, that deceiver said, 'After three days, I will arise.'

Note: It is remarkable that these enemies of Jesus remembered and understood what Jesus meant when he said he would rise from the dead in three days.

64. Therefore, command that the sepulcher be guarded until the third day, lest his disciples come at night and steal him away, and then tell the people, 'He has risen from the dead,' and so, the last delusion be worse than the first."

65. Pilate said to them, "You have a guard. Go make it as secure as you can."

66. Then they went with a guard and made the sepulcher secure, sealing the stone.

Note: Israel's leaders did not believe that Jesus would rise from the dead. They put a guard at the tomb to keep Jesus' followers from stealing his dead body and then claiming that he had risen.

Matthew 28

¶1. Then, after the Sabbath, at dawn on the first day of the week, Mary the Magdalene came with the other Mary to see the tomb.

Note: These women loved Jesus and would have stayed longer at his tomb the day he died, but it was late afternoon when he was buried, and the Sabbath was coming on. And they would have returned the next day, but they were forbidden to do so on the Sabbath. So, they had to wait until the third day to return. In His wisdom and love, God planned His Son's death so that these good women, who had followed and ministered to Jesus from his days in Galilee (Lk. 8:1–3), would be the first to see him when he rose from the dead.

2. And behold, there had been a great earthquake, for the angel of the LORD had descended from heaven. And when he came, he rolled the stone away from the entrance and sat on top of it.

3. His appearance was as lightning, and his clothing as white as snow,

4. and for fear of him, those keeping guard had trembled and had become like dead men.

5. But the angel answered and said to the women, "Don't be afraid. I know that *you're* looking for Jesus, who was crucified.

6. He's not here, for he is risen, just as he said. Come see the place where the Lord was laid.

7. And quickly now, go tell his disciples, 'He is raised from the dead, and, behold, he is going ahead of *you* into Galilee. There *you* will see him.' Behold, I have told *you*!"

8. And leaving the sepulcher quickly, with fear and great joy, they ran to tell his disciples.

9. But as they went to carry the message to his disciples, behold, Jesus met them, saying, "Good morning!"[2] And they came near and held his feet, and prostrated themselves before him.

---

[2] This is a casual greeting which meant something like, "Hello, there!", or even "Shalom!"

10. Then Jesus said to them, "Don't be afraid. Go on your way. Carry the message to my brothers, that they should leave for Galilee, and they will see me there."

¶11. Now, while the women were on the way, behold, some of the guard went into the city and reported to the chief priests everything that had happened.

12. And when they had gathered with the elders and taken counsel, they gave the soldiers a substantial amount of silver

13. and said, "You say, 'His disciples came by night and stole him as we slept.'

14. And if this is heard by the governor, we will persuade him and keep you out of trouble."

15. So, taking the money, they did as they were instructed. And this rumor is spread by the Jews to this day.

¶16. Then the eleven disciples went into Galilee, to the mountain to which Jesus had directed them.

17. And when they saw him, they bowed down to him, but some had their doubts.

Note 1: The women had told the disciples that they saw and spoke with Jesus, and now Jesus was standing right in front of them; yet, the disciples still struggled to believe.

Note 2: It is remarkable that Jesus' disciples had doubts about what they were experiencing (seeing Jesus alive again), but the soldiers who were guarding the sepulcher had no doubts at all about what they had experienced (seeing the angel).

18. And Jesus drew near and spoke to them, saying, "All authority in heaven and on earth is given to me.

19a. Go teach all nations,

Note: That the disciples understood Jesus to mean they should go to the Jews who lived in foreign nations, not to the Gentiles, is made obvious in Acts 10. There, God had to compel a very reluctant Peter to go preach to Gentiles. Jesus sent no one as an apostle to the Gentiles until he sent Paul and Barnabas (Acts 13:2; Gal. 2:1–10).

19b. baptizing them in the name of the Father, and of the Son, and of the holy Spirit,

20. teaching them to keep everything that I command *you*. And behold, I am with *you* always, *even* to the end of the world." Amen.

Note: Concerning the spiritual condition of Jesus' followers after Jesus died, Matthew is fairly neutral. He mentions the unbelief of the disciples only once, and that, briefly (Mt. 28:17). The other gospels, however, make it abundantly clear that the disciples had all given up hope in Jesus as their Messiah when he died.

End of Matthew

After Jesus Died in Mark

Mark 15

37. Then Jesus, letting out a great cry, breathed out *his* life.

38. And the veil of the temple was torn in two, from top to bottom.

39. Now, when the centurion, who had been standing out in front of him, saw him cry out like that and breathe out *his* life, he said, "This man really was a son of a god!"

40. And there were women looking on from a distance, among whom were also Mary the Magdalene, and Mary the mother of James the small and of Joses, and Salome.

41. These also, when he was in Galilee, followed him and ministered to him, along with many other women who came up with him to Jerusalem.

Question (repeated): Why were these women, righteous and good as they were, just "looking on from a distance," and not rejoicing that the debt for the whole world's sin was being paid and that man's redemption from bondage to his fallen, corrupt nature was at hand?

Answer: They were not aware that the debt for man's sin was being paid or that man even needed to be redeemed from a fallen nature.

¶42. And evening having already come, and since it was the Preparation, which is the day before the Sabbath,

43. Joseph of Arimathaea, a prominent member of the Council, who himself also was awaiting the kingdom of God, went and entered in boldly to Pilate and asked for Jesus' body.

Note (repeated): Joseph was probably ashamed of himself for fearing to confess his faith in Jesus while Jesus was alive (Jn. 19:38) and was now trying to make up for it by honoring Jesus publicly.

44. But Pilate was amazed that he was already dead, and he summoned the centurion and asked him if he had been dead long.
45. And when he had ascertained from the centurion *that it was so,* he granted the body to Joseph.
46. And when he had purchased linen cloth and taken him down, he wrapped him in the cloth and laid him in a sepulcher that had been hewn out of a rock, and then he rolled a stone upon the entrance of the sepulcher.

Note (repeated): Joseph would have done the same for anyone he loved. This manner of burial was not unusual among well-to-do Jews of the time; it does not suggest that Joseph was born again, or even that he possessed exceptional faith or knowledge of God. On the contrary, Joseph did not believe that Jesus would rise from the dead; otherwise, he would not have shrouded Jesus' body in burial linen.

47. And Mary the Magdalene and Mary the mother of Joses were observing where he was laid.

Note (repeated): Nothing in this verse indicates that these women were born again and believed that Jesus would rise from the dead. All that we are told here is that they attended Jesus' burial, which they would have done for anyone they loved.

Mark 16

Note: The following takes place on the third day after Jesus died, the day he foretold that he would rise from the dead.

¶1a. And when the Sabbath was past, Mary the Magdalene, and Mary the mother of James, and Salome,

Note (repeated): These women loved Jesus and would have stayed longer at his tomb the day he died, but it was late afternoon when he was buried, and the Sabbath was coming on. They would have returned the next day, but they were forbidden to do so on the Sabbath. So, they had to wait until the third day to return. In His wisdom and love, God planned His Son's death so that these good women, who had followed and ministered to Jesus from his days in

Galilee (Lk. 8:1–3), would be the first to see him when he rose from the dead.

1b. purchased fragrant oils that they might come and anoint him.

Note: The women purchased fragrant oils to pour on Jesus' corpse because they expected his dead body to decay in the tomb and begin to stink (cp. Jn. 11:39). They did not expect his body to come back to life and have no need for their odor-concealing perfumes.

2. And very early in the morning of the first day of the week, when the sun had risen, they came to the sepulcher.

Note: The women returned as soon as they could see well enough to do so on the third day.

3. And they were saying to each other, "Who will roll away the stone from the entrance of the sepulcher for us?"

Note 1: They expected nothing to have changed since the day Joseph put Jesus' crucified body in that tomb.

Note 2: These women wanted the stone moved so that they could enter the tomb, not so that Jesus could get out of it.

4. But when they looked up, they saw that the stone had been rolled away, though it was very large.

Note: The miracle is what God had done, not what they did. There was nothing miraculous about them looking up and seeing the stone rolled away.

5. And when they entered the sepulcher, they saw a young man, clothed in a long, white robe, sitting to their right, and they were alarmed.

6. But he said to them, "Do not be alarmed. You are looking for Jesus of Nazareth who was crucified. He is risen; he is not here. Behold the place where they laid him!

Note: These women did not rejoice at seeing God's angel and cry out, "Praise God! We knew Jesus would do it!" On the contrary, they were surprised and frightened because the thought did not even enter their minds that Jesus would rise from the dead.

7. But go your way. Tell his disciples, especially Peter, 'He is going ahead of you into Galilee. There you will see him, just as he told you.'"

8. And when they went out, they fled from the sepulcher, and trembling and amazement gripped them, and they said nothing to anyone, for they were afraid.

Note: The women did not run joyously down the road proclaiming to everyone they met, "Praise God! Jesus has come back from the dead, just as he said!" Instead, "they said nothing to anyone, for they were afraid." Jesus' resurrection astounded his followers; it did not, at first, thrill and delight them.

¶9. Now, after he arose, early in the morning the first day of the week, he appeared first to Mary the Magdalene, out of whom he had cast seven demons.

10. She was the one who went and gave the report to those who had been with him, *as* they were mourning and weeping.

Question: On this, the third day after Jesus died, why were Jesus' disciples still "mourning and weeping"?

Answer: They were still mourning and weeping because they did not believe that Jesus would rise from the dead.

11. And when they heard that he was alive and had been seen by her, they did not believe *it*.

Question: Why, even after hearing from an eyewitness that Jesus was risen, did the disciples not rejoice?

Answer: They were so certain that Jesus was permanently dead that they could not believe Mary Magdalene's report.

¶12. After these things, he appeared to two of them in another form as they were walking, going into the country.

Note: Even after Mary told the disciples that she had seen Jesus and that Jesus said for them to go meet him in Galilee, those two dejected disciples left Jerusalem, not to go to Galilee, but "into the country" to the city of Emmaus (Lk. 24:13, 17).

13. Then those men went and reported it to the rest, but they did not believe them, either.

Note: Even after hearing this report from two of their own, Jesus' disciples did not rejoice and say, "Mary must have been right! We should have believed her. Jesus is risen!" Far from it! They dismissed the report of these two fellow disciples, as well as Mary's.

– Consider This –

If Jesus' disciples had attempted to preach at this time, their message could only have been something like this: "We have heard rumors of Jesus rising from the dead, but we don't believe it."

To whom would such a message have appealed, except Caiaphas and others like him, who also didn't believe in the resurrection?

¶14. Afterward, he appeared to the eleven themselves as they reclined for a meal, and he rebuked their unbelief and hardness of heart because they did not believe those who had seen him after he had risen.

Note: It had been very early that resurrection morning when Jesus commanded Mary to tell his disciples to go to Galilee and meet them there. But because the disciples did not believe Mary, they were still huddled in their hiding place in Jerusalem (Jn. 20:19).

15. And he told them, "Go into all the world and preach the gospel to every creature.

Note (repeated): That the disciples understood Jesus to mean they should go to the Jews who lived in foreign nations, not to Gentiles, is made obvious in Acts 10. There, God had to compel a very reluctant Peter to go preach to Gentiles. Jesus sent no one as an apostle to the Gentiles until he sent Paul and Barnabas (Acts 13:2; Gal. 2:1–10).

16. He who believes and is baptized will be saved, but he who does not believe will be damned.

17. These signs will accompany those who believe: In my name, they will cast out demons; they will speak with new tongues;

18. they will take up serpents; and if they drink any deadly thing, it shall not hurt them; they will lay hands on the sick, and they shall recover."

Note: Other than when Jesus sent them out for a time to work miracles in his name (Mk. 6:7), the disciples did none of these things until after they received the Spirit at Pentecost.

¶19. Then the Lord, after he had spoken to them, was taken up into heaven, and he sat down at the right hand of God.

Note 1: This is Mark's version of Jesus' ascension, which took place in Acts 1.

Note 2: Mark's purpose was not to give an account of the acts of the apostles after their new birth, but only to tell the story of Jesus' work on earth. Therefore, he ends his book with the following very brief comment concerning the apostles after they were born of the Spirit in Acts 2 and were sent by God to preach the gospel.

20. And they went out preaching everywhere, the Lord working with them, confirming the word with signs that followed. **Amen.**

End of Mark

After Jesus Died in Luke

Luke 23

46. Jesus cried in a loud voice and said, "Father, into your hands I commit my spirit." And after saying these words, he breathed out *his* life.

47. Now, when the captain saw what happened, he honored God, saying, "Surely, this was a righteous man!"

48. And all the people who were gathered for this spectacle, watching the things that took place, began to go back, beating their breasts.

49. And all those who knew him stood far off to see these things, including the women who followed along with him from Galilee.

Question (repeated): Why were these women, righteous and good as they were, just "looking on from a distance," and not rejoicing that the debt for the whole world's sin was being paid and that man's redemption from bondage to his fallen, corrupt nature was at hand?

Answer: They were not aware that the debt for man's sin was being paid or that man even needed to be redeemed from a fallen nature.

¶50. And behold, there was a man named Joseph, a good and just man, a member of the Council

51. (he had not consented to their scheme or actions), from Arimathaea, a Jewish city, who himself also was awaiting the kingdom of God.

52. This man approached Pilate and asked for Jesus' body.

Note (repeated): Joseph was probably ashamed of himself for fearing to confess his faith in Jesus while Jesus was alive (Jn.

19:38) and was now trying to make up for it by honoring Jesus publicly.

53. And when he had taken it down, he wrapped it up in a linen cloth and laid it in a sepulcher hewn in stone, in which no one had ever yet been laid.

Note (repeated): Joseph would have done the same for anyone he loved. This manner of burial was not unusual among well-to-do Jews of the time; it does not suggest that Joseph was born again, or even that he possessed exceptional faith or knowledge of God. On the contrary, Joseph did not believe that Jesus would rise from the dead; otherwise, he would not have shrouded Jesus' body in burial linen.

54. And it was the day of Preparation; twilight was bringing in the Sabbath.

55. And women who had come with him from Galilee followed, and they observed the sepulcher and how his body was laid.

Note (repeated): Nothing in this verse indicates that these women were born again and believed that Jesus would rise from the dead. All that we are told here is that they attended Jesus' burial, which they would have done for anyone they loved.

56a. Then they returned and prepared spices and perfumes.

Note (repeated): The women prepared spices and perfumes for Jesus' corpse because they expected his dead body to decay in the tomb and begin to stink (cp. Jn. 11:39). They did not expect his body to come back to life and have no need for their odor-concealing perfumes.

56b. And they rested on the Sabbath, according to the commandment.

Note: These women loved Jesus and would have come to anoint his dead body with perfumes the day he died, but it was too late. Nor could they come back the next day with their perfumes, for it was the Sabbath. In His wisdom and love, God planned His Son's death so that these good women, who had followed and ministered to Jesus from his days in Galilee (Lk. 8:1–3), would have to wait until the third day to bring their spices to the tomb. God loved them and wanted them to be the first to see His Son when he rose.

Luke 24

Note: The following events take place on the third day after Jesus died.

¶1. Now, on the first *day* of the week, at the break of dawn, they came to the grave, bringing the spices which they had prepared, and some others were with them,

2. but they found the stone rolled away from the sepulcher.

Note: The women's discovery of the open tomb shows only that God loved them enough to have them there to discover the open tomb. It speaks well of their heart, but it does not mean that they were born again.

3. And when they entered, they did not find the body of the Lord Jesus.

4a. And it came to pass that, as they stood there, utterly perplexed,

Note: The women were perplexed because, in spite of hearing Jesus foretell on several occasions that he would rise from the dead on the third day, they could not imagine why, three days after he died, the tomb was empty.

4b. behold, two men in shining clothes were standing with them,

5. and they were afraid. And as they bowed, faces to the ground, he said to them, "Why do *you* seek the living among the dead?

6. He is not here; he is risen. Remember how he told *you*, when he was still in Galilee,

7. that the Son of man must be betrayed into the hands of wicked men and be crucified, and then rise from the dead on the third day."

8. And they remembered his words.

Note: They had to be reminded that Jesus told them he would suffer and die because they had never understood or believed what he told them.

9. And when they returned from the sepulcher, they reported all these things to the eleven, and to all the rest.

10. (They were the Magdalene Mary, and Joanna, and Mary the mother of James, and the other women with them, who told these things to the apostles.)

11. But their words seemed to them like idle talk, and they did not believe them.

Note: Jesus once sent these disciples out, for a short time, with power to heal the sick and raise the dead (Mt. 10:5–8). One would think that their experience with God's miracle-working power would have created within the disciples sufficient faith to believe those who now said they had seen the risen Lord, but it did not.

12. Nevertheless, Peter got up and ran to the sepulcher, and when he looked in, he saw the linen wrappings lying by themselves. And he went away, wondering to himself what had happened.

Note: It is remarkable that Peter was wondering what had happened, even though Jesus had repeatedly told him that the resurrection *would* happen, and even though people were telling him now that the resurrection *had* happened.

¶13. And on the same day, behold, two of them were traveling to a village named Emmaus, about sixty stadia[3] from Jerusalem,

Note 1: These two disciples left Jerusalem after Mary told them that she had seen Jesus and that Jesus said for them to go meet him in Galilee.

Note 2: As discouraged as these men were, they no doubt would have gone to Emmaus the day after Jesus died, but that was a Sabbath, and to walk that far was not allowed. One would think that they would at least have waited until the fourth day to leave town, just in case Jesus did rise from the dead, but they had absolutely no expectation of it; so, they left.

14. and they were conversing with one another about all these things that had happened.

---

[3] Sixty stadia is approximately seven miles.

15. And it came to pass that while they talked and reasoned together, Jesus himself drew near and walked with them.

16. But their eyes were kept from recognizing him.

17. Then he said to them, "What are these things that *you're* discussing as *you* go along, looking so sad?"

Note: These two men were sad, not because they had not yet seen the resurrected Jesus, but because they were thinking, as the following verses show, that their faith in Jesus as the Messiah had been in vain.

18. The one named Cleopas answered and said to him, "Are you the only one living near Jerusalem who doesn't know what things have happened in it these *past few* days?"

19. He said to them, "What things?" Then they said to him, "The things concerning Jesus of Nazareth, who was a man, a prophet, mighty in deed and word before God and all the people,

Note: Cleopas is no longer referring to Jesus as the Messiah, but only as a great prophet.

20. and how our chief priests and rulers handed him over *to the Gentiles* to be condemned to death, and they crucified him.

21a. We were hoping that he was the one who was going to redeem Israel.

Note: In other words, "We were hoping that Jesus was the Messiah, but they killed him; so, obviously, we were wrong."

21b. And now, after all these things – today marks the third day since these things happened –

Note: Again, these men had left Jerusalem, not waiting to see if Jesus would rise on the third day, as he had often told them he would do. The fact that this was the third day after Jesus died meant nothing to them.

22. some of the women among us utterly astounded us when, after going to the sepulcher early in the morning

23. and not finding his body, they came *back* saying that they had actually seen a vision of angels who said he was alive!

Note: This last statement was not factually true. The women did *not* tell the disciples they had seen a *vision* of angels; they told them they had *really* seen angels. However, the disciples, unable to believe their report, apparently decided that it must have only been a vision that the women saw.

24. And then some of those with us went out to the sepulcher and found it exactly as the women said, but they didn't see him."

Note: So, even though certain facts of the women's story had been confirmed for these disciples, they were still heavy with sadness as they walked down the road together. This tells us that they were not even entertaining the possibility that Jesus had risen from the dead.

25. Then he said to them, "O foolish men, so slow in heart to believe all that the prophets have spoken!
26. Didn't the Messiah have to suffer these things and enter into his glory?"

Note: Though Jesus had died and come back from the dead, the spiritual condition of his disciples was not changed. The resurrection had taken place, but it had not affected them at all. Jesus called them foolish because they were still as blind to the things of God as they had always been.

27. And beginning with Moses and all the prophets, he began explaining to them the things concerning himself in all the scriptures.

Note: Explaining the scriptures to someone does not make that person born again. Multitudes have had the scriptures explained to them without being born of God.

28. And they drew near the village where they were going, and he made as though he was going farther,
29. but they prevailed upon him, saying, "Stay with us. It's nearly evening; the day is far spent." And so, he went in to lodge with them.

Note: They invited him to spend the night because they were hospitable, not because they were born again.

30. And it came to pass as he ate with them that he took the bread and blessed it, and then he broke it and gave it to them.
31. Then their eyes were opened, and they recognized him, but he vanished from their sight.
32. And they said to one another, "Wasn't our heart burning within us while he was talking with us on the road, and while he was explaining the scriptures to us?"
33a. And they arose the same hour and returned to Jerusalem,

Note: It was late in the afternoon when Jesus appeared to these two disciples (v. 29), and after their lengthy visit with him, including the evening meal, they had to walk seven miles back to Jerusalem. Their arrival in Jerusalem, then, must have been after dark.

33b. and they found the eleven and those with them gathered together,
34. and they said, "The Master really has been raised up, and he was seen by Simon!"[4]
35. And they began detailing what happened on the road, and how he was made known to them in the breaking of the bread.
¶36. As they were telling these things, Jesus himself stood in their midst, and he said to them, "Peace to *you.*"
37. But they were startled and afraid, thinking they were seeing a ghost.

Note 1: It was after dark; the disciples' hearts were still broken because of Jesus' death; they were living in fear and hiding behind locked doors from the rulers of the Jews; and now, a figure suddenly appeared in their midst, in the flickering light of their candles. It was enough to make them think they were seeing a ghost, but it was not enough to make them believe that Jesus was alive from the dead.

---

[4] No gospel tells of Jesus talking with Peter the morning he rose from the dead. How they learned of this, or if it was even true, we cannot say.

Note 2: The disciples did not believe either the women who saw Jesus after his resurrection or the two disciples who returned to Jerusalem to tell them about seeing him (Mk. 16:13). And now, in this scene, they do not even believe their own eyes!

– Consider This –

If Jesus' disciples had attempted to preach at this time, what could they have preached but something like this: "We have heard some rumors about Jesus rising from the dead, but we don't believe it. We ourselves longed to see Jesus again so much that we even saw his ghost, or perhaps it was a vision of him. But we know, of course, that Jesus is not really alive."

To whom would such a message have appealed, except Caiaphas and others like him, who hated Jesus and had schemed to have him crucified?

38. And he said to them, "Why are *you* troubled? And why do doubts come up in *your* hearts?

Note: It is easy to read over this and not pause to consider that Jesus is speaking to his closest disciples. Jesus' appearance in their midst "troubled" them; it did not bless them. Doubts arose in their hearts, not joy and relief. Would born-again ministers of God react like that to the resurrected Savior?

39. See my hands and my feet, that it is me. Touch me and see! A ghost doesn't have flesh and bones the way *you* see I have."
40. And after he said this, he presented *his* hands and feet to them.

Note: Jesus told them to touch him because they did not yet believe he was real, and he knew that some physical evidence would help them to believe.

41. But while they still disbelieved for joy, and were amazed, he said to them, "Do *you* have any food here?"

Note: Even after touching him, the disciples had difficulty believing he was real, so Jesus decided to eat something, to prove to them that he really was back in his natural body, able to eat natural food the way they did. Ghosts cannot do that.

42. And they gave him a piece of broiled fish and some honeycomb.
43. And he took *it,* and ate in their presence.
44. And then he said to them, "These are the words that I spoke to *you* while I was yet with *you,* that everything written about me in the law of Moses, and in the prophets, and in Psalms must be fulfilled."

Note: In other words, "Why are you amazed? I told you that all these things would happen."

45. Then he opened their mind to understand the scriptures,
46. and he said to them, "Thus it is written, and so, it was necessary for the Messiah to suffer and to rise from the dead on the third day,

Note: Having their "minds opened to understand the scriptures" does not mean that the disciples were born again. It means only that Jesus was helping them to understand *everything* that the scriptures said about their Messiah, not just the glorious parts. The Jews, including Jesus' disciples, had never understood or believed the prophecies of the Messiah's sufferings, only those of his glory. Jesus opened their minds to understand and to believe all that the prophets had foretold.

47. and for repentance and remission of sins to be preached in his name to all nations, beginning in Jerusalem.

Note (repeated): That the disciples understood Jesus to mean they should go to the Jews who lived in foreign nations, not to Gentiles, is made obvious in Acts 10. There, God had to compel a very reluctant Peter to go preach to Gentiles. Jesus sent no one as an apostle to the Gentiles until he sent Paul and Barnabas (Acts 13:2; Gal. 2:1–10).

48. Now, *you* are witnesses of these things.

Note: The events summarized in verses 48–53 are recorded in more detail in Acts 2 and beyond.

49a. And, behold, I am sending the promise of my Father upon *you*.

49b. As for *you*, *you* stay in the city of Jerusalem until *you* be clothed with power from on high!"

Note 1: The Spirit is "the promise of the Father" (Gal. 3:14; Eph. 1:13; Heb. 11:39), and it makes no sense for Jesus to tell his disciples to go wait in Jerusalem for the Spirit if they already had it.

Note 2: Previously, when Jesus commanded them to go to Galilee to meet him, the disciples did not have enough faith to leave Jerusalem for more than a week (Jn. 20:19, 26). Now, however, though the disciples did not understand what receiving the Spirit meant, they had regained enough faith in Jesus to be able to obey him and go wait in the city of Jerusalem for it.

¶50. Then he led them out as far as Bethany, and then he lifted up his hands and blessed them.

Note: This was Jesus' parting blessing for his beloved disciples; it was not their new birth.

51. And it came to pass as he was blessing them that he parted from them and was carried up into heaven.

52. And they worshipped him and returned to Jerusalem with great joy,

Note: The disciples were rejoicing because they finally be-lieved that Jesus was alive and, as later events show, because they were expecting him to soon return. Their joy does not mean they were now born-again.

53. and they were continually in the temple, praising and blessing God. Amen.

Note: The disciples were not bold enough to "continually be in the temple praising and blessing God" before the Spirit came, mak-ing them "new creatures in Christ Jesus". Until then, they stayed out of sight in their hiding place in Jerusalem (cp. Jn. 20:19).

End of Luke

After Jesus Died in John

John 19

30. When Jesus received the wine vinegar, he said, "It is finished." And bowing his head, he gave up the spirit.

¶31. Now, since it was the Preparation, and so that the bodies would not remain on the cross on the Sabbath (for that Sabbath was a high day), the Jews requested of Pilate that their legs be broken and they be taken away.

32. Then the soldiers came and broke the legs of the first man and of the other who was crucified with him,

33. but when they came to Jesus, they did not break his legs, seeing he was dead already.

34. Nevertheless, one of the soldiers pierced his side with his spear, and blood and water immediately came out.

35. And he who saw this has borne witness – and his testimony is true, and he knows that he is speaking truthfully – so that *you* might believe.

Note: Until John received the Spirit on the day of Pentecost, John could not have written the two explanatory verses which follow, for at the time of the crucifixion, he did not understand what God was doing in Christ.

36. These things happened so that the scripture might be fulfilled: "Not a bone of his shall be broken."

37. And again, another scripture says, "They will look upon him whom they pierced."

¶38a. After these things, Joseph who was from Arimathaea, a disciple of Jesus, but secretly because of fear of the Jews, asked Pilate if he could take away the body of Jesus.

Note (repeated): Joseph was probably ashamed of himself for fearing to confess his faith in Jesus while Jesus was alive and was now trying to make up for it by honoring Jesus publicly.

38b. And Pilate gave *him* permission. So, he came and took Jesus' body away.

39. And Nicodemus, who at the first came to Jesus by night, also came, bringing a mixture of myrrh and aloe, about one hundred pounds.

40. So they took the body of Jesus and bound it in linen sheets with the spices, as is the burial custom of the Jews.

Note: Joseph and Nicodemus shrouded Jesus' body in linen and one hundred pounds of spices because they did *not* believe he would rise from the dead. They were expecting his body to decay.

41. Now, there was in the place where he was crucified a garden, and in the garden a new sepulcher in which no man had yet been laid.

42. There they laid Jesus, since it was the Jews' Preparation and the sepulcher was close by.

Note (repeated): Joseph would have done the same for anyone he dearly loved. This manner of burial was not unusual among well-to-do Jews of the time; it does not suggest that Joseph was born again, or even that he possessed extraordinary faith or the knowledge of God. On the contrary, Joseph did not believe that Jesus would rise from the dead; like everyone else who loved Jesus, Joseph thought Jesus was dead and gone.

John 20

1. Then, early on the first day of the week, while it was still dark, Mary the Magdalene came to the sepulcher and saw that the stone was removed from the sepulcher.

2. So she ran and came to Simon Peter and another disciple (the one whom Jesus loved), and she said to them, "They've taken the Lord out of the sepulcher, and we don't know where they've put him."

Note 1: Upon seeing the open door of the tomb, even on this third day after Jesus' crucifixion, Mary's first thought was not that

Jesus had risen from the dead but that somebody had stolen his dead body. That reaction to seeing the open tomb shows that Mary had not come to see if Jesus had risen, but to mourn.

Note 2: Matthew told us that some of Jesus' enemies expected his disciples to steal Jesus' body in order to make it appear that he had risen from the dead (Mt. 27:64). When Mary saw the stone rolled away from the tomb, she ran and told the disciples that somebody had stolen Jesus' body and "we don't know where they've put him" (vv. 1–2). Peter then ran to the tomb, but when he looked in, he wondered why it was empty (Lk. 24:12). And when Mary returned to the tomb, she asked the "gardener" if he was the one who did it (Jn. 20:15). Had Jesus not revealed himself to his followers, a controversy would no doubt have erupted between them and Jesus' enemies concerning which group stole Jesus' body out of the tomb. Nobody on either side believed that Jesus had risen from the dead, except, possibly, the Roman soldiers who were guarding the tomb when God's angel descended from heaven – and the rulers of the Jews paid them to keep quiet about it (Mt. 28:11–15).

3. Then Peter went out, and the other disciple, and they went to the sepulcher.
4. Now, the two men started out running together, but the other disciple quickly outran Peter and came to the sepulcher first,
5. and bending over to look, he saw the linen cloths lying there, though he did not actually enter.
6. Then Simon Peter came, following him, and went into the sepulcher, and saw the linen cloths lying there
7. and the face cloth that was on his head, not laid with the linen cloths, but folded up in a place by itself.
8. So then the other disciple entered, the one who came to the sepulcher first, and he saw, and believed.

Note: John, "the other disciple", was the first of the disciples to believe that Jesus was risen.

9. (No one had yet understood the scripture, that he had to rise from the dead.)

Note: Not only had no one yet understood the scriptures about the Messiah rising from the dead, neither had anyone understood Jesus who had told them the same thing while he was alive.

10. Then the disciples went back to their *friends.*

¶11a. But Mary stood outside by the sepulcher weeping,

Note: John obviously did not confess to the grieving Mary that he was persuaded that Jesus was risen, but even if he had done so, she may not yet have been able to believe him.

11b. and as she wept, she bent over to look into the sepulcher,

12. and she saw two angels in white sitting where the body of Jesus had lain, one at the head and one at the foot.

13. And they said to her, "Woman, why are you crying?" She said to them, "Because they've taken my Lord away, and I don't know where they've put him."

Note: Mary was so consumed by grief because of her assumption that Jesus' body had been stolen that she did not realized she was speaking to angels. Obviously, the possibility that Jesus had risen from the dead had not entered into Mary's mind.

14. And when she had said these things, she turned around and saw Jesus standing there, but she did not know that it was Jesus.

15. Jesus said to her, "Woman, why are you crying? Who are you looking for?" She, assuming that he was the gardener, said to him, "Sir, if you have removed him, tell me where you put him, and I will take him away."

16. Jesus said to her, "Mary." And turning around, she said to him, "Rabbi!" (which means "Teacher").

Note: Before Jesus died, Mary spent much time with him and knew his voice well. But she so little expected to ever hear his voice again that, here, she did not recognize his voice until he spoke to her the second time.

17. Jesus said to her, "Don't cling to me, for I haven't yet ascended to my Father. But go to my brothers and tell them, 'I am ascending to my Father and *your* Father, and to my God and *your* God.'"

18. Mary the Magdalene went and reported to the disciples that she had seen the Lord and he said these things to her.

¶19a. When it was evening on that day, the first day of the week, although the doors were locked where the disciples were gathered because of fear of the Jews, Jesus came and stood in the midst and said to them, "Peace to *you*."

Note: Very early that day, both Jesus and an angel had sent Mary with a message to the disciples, for them to go to Galilee, where Jesus would meet them (Mt. 28:10; Mk. 16:7).   But it was now growing dark and the disciples were still in Jerusalem, hiding. They were not on their way to Galilee.   Much less were they out preaching, trying to win unbelieving souls; instead, Jesus was trying to win back *their* unbelieving souls.

20. And after he said this, he showed them his hands and his side. Then the disciples rejoiced at seeing the Lord.

Note: It is only here, after seeing the marks of Jesus' crucifixion, that the disciples began to believe that Jesus was really risen.

21. Then Jesus said to them again, "Peace to *you*.   As the Father has sent me, so am I sending *you*."

Note: In saying this, Jesus did not mean that he was sending the disciples out to preach the gospel *that very minute*.   He meant only that he would be sending them very soon.

22. And after he said this, he breathed out and said to them, "Receive *the* holy Spirit.

23. If *you* forgive the sins of any, they are forgiven them; whose *you* retain are retained."

Note: Jesus did not mean that he was giving the disciples the holy Spirit and authority to forgive sins at that moment.   He had not yet even ascended into heaven to offer the sacrifice which would make the Spirit available to them.[5]   Jesus meant only that they would soon receive the Spirit and its power.

---

[5] For more on this, see chapter two, "The Sacrifice of Christ", in my online book, *Spiritual Light*, at GoingtoJesus.com.

¶24. But one of the twelve, Thomas, who is called Didymus[6], was not with them when Jesus came.

25. Therefore, the other disciples told him, "We have seen the Lord!" But he said to them, "Unless I see the mark of the nails in his hands, and stick my finger into the mark of the nails, and stick my hand into his side, I will never believe!"

Question: What, exactly, was Thomas saying he would never believe?

Answer: First, Thomas was saying that he would never believe that Jesus was alive again. It necessarily follows that he was also saying he would never believe that Jesus was Israel's Redeemer, for a dead man could not be the Messiah. Thomas was expressing the same sentiment expressed by the two disciples Jesus met on the road to Emmaus: "We were hoping that he was the one who was going to redeem Israel" (Lk. 24:21).

Note: Thomas was so certain that Jesus would not come back from the dead that for over a week (see next verse), he did not believe in the resurrection even when the other disciples told him they had seen Jesus, though they must have been telling him the whole time that Jesus was indeed alive again.

¶26a. Then, eight days later, his disciples were again inside, and Thomas with them. Jesus came, the doors being locked,

Note: The disciples were still hiding behind locked doors in Jerusalem; they were not at this point "continually in the temple, praising and blessing God" (Lk 24:53). They had not even yet obeyed Jesus and gone to Galilee. Maybe they were waiting to convince Thomas before they left. At any rate, to help Thomas appears to be the principal reason Jesus appeared to them again.

26b. and he stood in the midst and said, "Peace to *you*."

27. Then he said to Thomas, "Bring your finger here, and behold my hands, and bring your hand and stick it into my side. And don't be faithless, but believing."

28. Then Thomas answered and said to him, "My Lord and my God!"

---

[6] That is, "Twin".

29. Jesus said to him, "Because you have seen me, you have believed? Blessed are they who have not seen and yet believe."

Note: Only after this do the disciples go to Galilee.

¶30. Now, to be sure, Jesus, in the presence of his disciples, performed many other miracles as well which are not written in this book.

31. But these things are written so that *you* might believe that Jesus is the Messiah, the Son of God, and that believing, *you* might have life in his name.

Note: Remember, John wrote this Gospel *after* he became a new creature in Christ on Pentecost morning. Verses 30 and 31 are expressions of the faith that John possessed only after he was born again.

John 21

¶1. After these things, Jesus showed himself again to the disciples by the Sea of Tiberias,[7] and this is how he showed *himself:*

Note: It is only after Jesus personally appeared to the disciples twice in Jerusalem, over a period of eight days, that they at last became willing to believe that if they traveled to Galilee, Jesus would meet them there.

2. Simon Peter, and Thomas, who is called Didymus, and Nathaniel, who was of Cana in Galilee, and the sons of Zebedee, and two other of his disciples were together.

3. Simon Peter said to them, "I'm going fishing." And they said to him, "We're coming with you, too." They went out immediately and boarded the boat, but they caught nothing that night.

Note: Peter's attitude and conduct here differs greatly from the days following Pentecost, when he refused to cease preaching so that he could perform menial tasks (Acts 6:1–4). Paul asked the rhetorical question, "How can men preach unless they are sent?" (Rom. 10:15). The obvious answer is, "They cannot." And

---

[7] The Sea of Tiberias is the Sea of Galilee.

it is because Jesus had not yet sent these disciples that they were fishing in Galilee instead of preaching the gospel.

4. And just as day was breaking, Jesus stood on the shore; however, the disciples did not know it was Jesus.

5. Then Jesus said to them, "Children, *you* didn't catch anything to eat, did *you*?" They answered him, "No."

6. Then he said to them, "Cast the net on the right side of the ship, and *you*'ll find *something*." So, they cast, but then they could not haul it in because of the multitude of fish.

7. Then that disciple whom Jesus loved said to Peter, "It's the Lord!" When Simon Peter heard that it was the Lord, he tied on his coat, for he was naked, and threw himself into the sea.[8]

8. But the other disciples came in the little boat (for they were not far from land, but only about two hundred cubits), dragging the net of fish.

9. Then, when they got out onto shore, they saw a coal fire was laid, and a fish laid on it, and bread.

10. Jesus said to them, "Bring some of the fish that *you* just caught."

11. Simon Peter came up and dragged the net onto land, filled with one hundred fifty-three large fish, and although there were so many, the net was not torn.

12. Jesus said to them, "Come and dine." And knowing that it was the Lord, not one of the disciples dared to ask him, "Who are you?"

Note: This comment by John shows that the disciples wanted to ask Jesus who he was, just to make sure, but lacked the courage to do so. Most likely, they dreaded hearing him berate them as fools again if they questioned again who he really was or whether he was a ghost.

13. So, Jesus came and took the bread and gave *it* to them, and likewise the fish.

14. (This was now the third time Jesus appeared to his disciples after he was raised from the dead.)

---

[8] Peter was not attempting suicide. He was going ashore.

¶15a. Then, when they had eaten, Jesus said to Simon Peter, "Simon, son of Jonah, do you love me more than these men *do?*"

Note: Jesus used a word for love that implies, in this context, a pure, steadfast, and holy love, the kind of love brought into the human heart by the holy Spirit (Rom. 5:5).

15b. He said to him, "Surely, Lord, you know that I'm your friend."

Note: The word Peter used for "love" differed from the word Jesus used. Peter's word for love referred to the love friends have for one another, not the holy love implied in the word Jesus used. Jesus was testing Peter to see if he would still put on an act of supreme self-confidence, as he had done before (Mt. 26:31–35), and by using a different word for love, Peter passed the test. He did not vaunt himself, boasting that he had a greater love for the Lord than did the other disciples, who had come to shore with Peter, and were no doubt listening to this conversation.

15c. He said to him, "Feed my lambs."

16a. Again, he said to him a second time, "Simon, son of Jonah, do you love me?"

Note: Jesus again used the word that implied a pure, holy love.

16b. *Peter* said to him, "Surely, Lord, you know that I'm your friend."

Note: Peter again passed the test, using the word for the love of a friend.

16b. He said to him, "Tend my sheep."

17a. The third time, he said to him, "Simon, son of Jonah, are you my friend?"

Note: This time, Jesus asked Peter if he even had a friend's kind of love for him.

17b. Peter was grieved because the third time, he said to him, "Are you my friend?" And he said to him, "Lord, you know all things; you know that I'm your friend."

Note: Though no longer boastful, Peter could not bring himself to say that he did not have even a friend's love for Jesus, and it grieved him that Jesus would even question that he did.

17c. Jesus said to him, "Feed my sheep.

18. Truly, truly, I tell you, when you were young, you dressed yourself and went where you wanted, but when you grow old, you'll stretch out your hands and another will dress you, and he will carry you where you don't want to go."

19. (He said this indicating by what kind of death he would glorify God.) And after he said this, he told him, "Follow me."

Note: John does not mention it, but here, Jesus walked away from the disciples gathered around the campfire, and Peter obediently followed him.

20. Then, when Peter turned around, he saw the disciple whom Jesus loved following (the one who also leaned on his chest during the supper and said, "Lord, who is the one who will betray you?")

21. When Peter saw him, he said to Jesus, "Lord, what about him?"

22. Jesus said to him, "If I want him to remain until I come, what is that to you? You follow me."

23. Then this rumor spread among the brothers, that that disciple would not die. But Jesus did not tell him that he would not die; rather, "If I want him to remain until I come, what is that to you?"

¶24. This is the disciple who is testifying about these things and wrote these things, and we know that his testimony is true.

¶25. There are also a great many other things Jesus did, which, if each one were written, I suppose that not even the world itself could contain the books which would be written. Amen.

Note: Of course, John wrote these final verses after he was born again at Pentecost and came to understand what God had done through His Son Jesus.

End of John

After Jesus Died, from Acts

Acts 1

¶1. The first account, O Theophilus, I have made concerning all the things Jesus both did and taught

2. up to the day that he was taken up, after he had given instructions through the holy Spirit to the apostles whom he had chosen,

3. to whom, after his suffering, he also presented himself alive by many convincing proofs, appearing to them over a period of forty days and speaking of things concerning the kingdom of God.

4. And being assembled together with them, he commanded them not to leave Jerusalem but to await the promise of the Father, "which", *he said,* "you have heard about from me.[9]

5. John indeed baptized with water, but *y*ou will be baptized with holy Spirit not many days from now."

¶6. When they had come together, they kept asking him, saying, "Master, is this the time you will re-establish the kingdom of Israel?"

Note: The disciples did not yet understand what Jesus once told them: "The kingdom of God is within *y*ou" (Lk. 17:20–21). They were still expecting Jesus to set up an earthly kingdom and to become king of the world, which he will do only when he returns. For Jesus to become king of the world before the appointed time was what Satan had once tempted Jesus to be (Mt. 4:8–9).

7. He said to them, "It isn't for *y*ou to know times or seasons which the Father has reserved to His own authority.

---

[9] A few instances of Jesus telling them that the Spirit would come are found in John 14:25–26, 15:26, and 16:7–14.

8. But *you* will receive power after the holy Spirit comes upon *you*, and *you* will be my witnesses, both in Jerusalem and in all Judea and Samaria, even to the uttermost part of the earth."

Note (repeated): That the disciples understood Jesus to mean they should go to the Jews who lived in foreign nations, not to Gentiles, is made obvious in Acts 10. There, God had to compel a very reluctant Peter to go preach to Gentiles. Jesus sent no one as an apostle to the Gentiles until he sent Paul and Barnabas (Acts 13:2; Gal. 2:1–10).

9. And when he had said these things, as they looked on, he was lifted up, and a cloud took him up out of their sight.
10. And he went away as they were gazing toward the sky, and then, behold, two men in white garments appeared to them,
11. and they said, "Men of Galilee, why are *you* standing there, staring at the sky? This same Jesus who was taken up from *you* into heaven will come *again,* the same way *you* watched him go into heaven."

Note: Thus far in the book of Acts, the disciples' part has been only to ask Jesus if it was time for him to become king of the world, and to look on as Jesus ascended into heaven, and then to stand there, gazing up into heaven after he was gone. All the miraculous parts of the story are still God's.

¶12. Then they returned to Jerusalem from the mountain called Olives, which is near Jerusalem, a Sabbath day's journey.
13. And when they had entered the city, they went up to the upper room where they were staying: Peter and James and John and Andrew, Philip and Thomas, Bartholomew and Matthew, James the son of Alphaeus and Simon the Patriot, and Judas the son of James.
14. These all, in one accord, continued in prayer and supplication, along with women, including Mary, Jesus' mother, and with his brothers.

Note: These men and women now had regained sufficient faith to obey Jesus' command to go back to Jerusalem and wait for the

Spirit, though they did not know what would happen when it came. They knew that Jesus said they would receive the Spirit, but they had no knowledge of what receiving the Spirit meant.

¶15. And during those days, Peter stood up in the midst of the disciples and said (the number of people there was about one hundred twenty),

16. "Men and brothers, this scripture must be fulfilled, which the holy Spirit foretold through the mouth of David concerning Judas, who was guide for those who arrested Jesus,

17. for he was numbered among us and obtained a part in this ministry.

18. (Afterward, with the reward of unrighteousness, this man purchased a field, but then, falling headlong, he burst open in the middle, and all his bowels spilled out.

19. And this became so well known by everyone living in Jerusalem that the field was called, in their own language, 'Akeldama', which means, 'field of blood'.)

20. For it is written in the book of Psalms, 'Let his home become desolate, and let there be no one living in it,' and, 'May another take his place.'

Note: Peter understood that this psalm spoke of Judas' betrayal of Jesus only because Jesus had opened his mind to understand and to believe everything the prophets had said about him. Peter was not yet born again, for the Spirit had not yet come.

21. It must be, then, that from among the men who accompanied us the entire time the Lord Jesus went in and out among us,

22. beginning from the baptism of John until the day that he was taken up from us, one of them should be made a witness of his resurrection with us."

23. And so, they put forward two: Joseph, the one called Barsabbas, who was surnamed Justus, and Matthias.

24. And they prayed and said, "You, LORD, knower of all hearts, show which one of these two you have chosen

25. to receive the part of this ministry and apostleship from which Judas turned to go to his own place."

26. Then they cast their lots, and the lot fell on Matthias, and so, he was numbered with the eleven apostles.

Note: Nothing else is ever said about this man, Matthias. This method of choosing an apostle may have been of God, but we should note that this is the only known case of an apostle being chosen by casting lots.

– Consider This –

Even if Jesus' disciples had attempted to preach at this time, their conversations with the people could only have been like this: "We have seen Jesus! He is risen from the dead! If you go look, you will find his empty tomb!"

But many of their listeners would have replied, "We've heard that you men stole Jesus' corpse out of the tomb so that you can claim he has risen from the dead. Where is he, if he is alive?"

"He has gone up into heaven. With our own eyes, we saw him ascend into the clouds!"

"Anybody can say that. How do we know that you are telling us the truth?"

"Well, you just have to take it by faith."

Whom would the disciples have won with that message, but gullible and unstable souls?

Note: Believing what others say, even if what they say is true, is not a secure foundation for the body of Christ. The body of Christ is securely built up by the word of God, not by the word of men (cp. Mt. 16:17–18). As John would later write, "If we receive the witness of men, the witness of God is greater" (1Jn. 5:9a).

The holy Spirit is the Father's witness to His Son (1Jn. 5:6b), and God's pouring out of that witness upon Jesus' followers, transforming them into born-again, living witnesses for His Son, is the epochal event which took place next, on the day of Pentecost.

Acts 2

¶1. When the day of Pentecost was fully come, they were all in one accord, in one place.

2. And suddenly there came a sound from heaven like a violent, rushing wind, and it filled the whole house where they were sitting.

3. And there appeared to them divided tongues like fire, and it sat upon each one of them,

4. and they were all filled with holy Spirit, and they began to speak in other tongues as the Spirit moved them to speak.

Note: This is the moment when the disciples were born again and became "new creatures in Christ Jesus". If we were to continue with our color scheme through the rest of the book of Acts, then the disciples' words and deeds would be marked in red, just as Jesus' words and deeds have been, for from the day of Pentecost, Christ was in them, and they, in him.

– Consider This –

When Jesus' disciples began preaching after this experience, their message was this: "Let all the house of Israel know assuredly that God has made Jesus both Lord and Messiah – this Jesus whom you crucified! Repent and be baptized, every one of you, in the name of Jesus Christ for the forgiveness of sins, and you will receive the gift of the holy Spirit! The promise is to you and to your children, and to all who are far off, as many as the LORD our God shall call."

Their message was also this: "He is the stone that was rejected by you builders, which has become the head of the corner. And salvation is not by any other, for there is no other name given among men by which we must be saved!"

And this: "The God of our fathers has raised up Jesus, whom you killed, hanging him on a tree. Him God has exalted to His right hand to be Prince and Savior, to give repentance to Israel, and forgiveness of sins. And we are his witnesses of these things, and so is the holy Spirit, which God has given to those who obey Him."

With that message and the power of the Spirit, the disciples won every soul whom God called into His kingdom.

End of Acts

Conclusion

The following are observations, based solely on the scriptures, concerning the words and deeds of Jesus' followers after he died, but before they received the Spirit on the day of Pentecost:

- When Jesus died, none of his followers rejoiced that Jesus had paid the debt for man's sin by his sacrificial death.
- When Jesus died, his followers thought they had been mistaken to believe he was the Messiah.
- None of Jesus' followers went to Jesus' tomb on the third day to see him rise from the dead.
- When Jesus appeared to Mary Magdalene at the tomb, she did not recognize his voice because she did not expect him to come back to life.
- When Jesus appeared to some women and told them to go tell his disciples that he was alive, they went and told the disciples, but the disciples dismissed their report as "idle talk".
- When Jesus appeared to two of his disciples on the road to Emmaus, they had lost all hope in him as Israel's Messiah, and only spoke of him as a great prophet.
- When Jesus appeared to his eleven disciples, they thought they were seeing a ghost.
- Thomas was not there when Jesus appeared to the other disciples, and he refused to believe even them when they told him Jesus had appeared to them.
- Later, when Jesus' disciples met him in Galilee, they still had doubts.

What is written in the Gospels concerning Jesus' followers after his death can teach us much about their spiritual condition; however, what is *not* written can teach us just as much. My notes were intended to bring out what is *not* written in order to emphasize what is often overlooked, in particular, the fact that Jesus' followers lost all faith in him as Messiah after he died. Thankfully, their faith was resurrected soon after Jesus was.

After his resurrection, Jesus rebuked his disciples for not believing *everything* that the prophets had said about him (Lk. 24:25, 44). They, and all the Jews, believed the prophecies concerning the Messiah's glory and triumph, but nobody in Israel believed the prophecies concerning his suffering and death. To this day, Jewish teachers demand that because he suffered and died, Jesus cannot be the Messiah. For example, the famed Jewish philosopher Maimonides (1135–1204) wrote, "If a king arises from the house of David, learned in the Torah and an observer of the commandments, as was David his father . . . and if he compels all of Israel to live according to it and to reinforce breaches in it, and if he fights the wars of the LORD, then it is this man, assuredly, who is Messiah. Once he has successfully accomplished *these things,* and has rebuilt the Sanctuary in its place, and has gathered the dispersed of Israel – then this man is certainly Messiah. And he will put the world aright – all of it – to serve the Name together.... But if he does not succeed in these things, or if he is killed, then this man is definitely not the one whom Torah promised.... Jesus the Nazarite thought he was Messiah indeed, but he was executed by the Council.'"[10] Before the disciples were born again on the day of Pentecost, Maimonides could have been speaking for them as well as the Jews who had rejected Jesus, for they all thought that way.

Neither those who loved Jesus nor those who hated him understood him while he was among them. The truth about God and His Son comes only through the Spirit (Jn. 16:13), and the Spirit was not yet given (Jn. 7:39). Therefore, those who loved Jesus while he labored on earth remained with him principally because of what they felt. It was only after Jesus rose from the dead, ascended, and was glorified by the Father that the Spirit came and enabled Jesus' followers to understand him.

It can hardly be over-emphasized that if Jesus' disciples had attempted to preach in the days immediately following Jesus' crucifixion, they could only have proclaimed this: "Give ear, O Israel! We have heard some women say Jesus has come back from

---

[10] Maimonides, *Hilkoth Melakhim* (excerpts, XI, 4).

the dead, but that is just idle talk." Or this: "O people of Israel, hear us! We used to believe Jesus was the Messiah, but he was killed; so, obviously, we were wrong." Or even this: "We have examined the tomb, and it is empty, just as some of our friends have said. But we don't know what to make of that." Even Jesus' enemies would have subscribed to the gospel which the disciples could have proclaimed before the day of Pentecost. And for a while, even after Jesus personally visited them, they remained confused and doubtful. That is why the disciples remained quiet and out of sight until they were born of the Spirit.

The apostle Paul gave us the simplest and best definition of being born again when he wrote, "If anyone does not have the Spirit of Christ, he does not belong to him" (Rom. 8:9). So, the question, "When were the disciples born again" is just another way of asking, "When did the disciples receive the Spirit?" The fact that they received the Spirit on the day of Pentecost is obvious to anyone whose mind is not befogged by a doctrinal prejudice. Such confusing fog has affected all of our minds to one extent or another, but it is completely dissipated by the bright, warm truth revealed by the Son of God.

Please let us know if you felt that sweet, heavenly influence as you read this book. And if you want more understanding of how the sacrifice of Christ was accomplished so that the disciples had to wait until Pentecost to receive the Spirit, it can be found in the second chapter of my book, *Spiritual Light*. Hard copies are available for purchase, or if you prefer, you may download and read *Spiritual Light* free of charge at GoingtoJesus.com.

To order your hard copy of *Spiritual Light*, send $4 to:

The Pioneer Tract Society
P. O. Box 99
Burlington, NC 27216-0099

Appendix

The Spiritual Condition of the Disciples
until the Day of Pentecost

1. They were clean (Jn. 13:10–11; 15:3), but before Pentecost, they were not sanctified (Jn. 17:17, 19).

2. They believed in God (Jn. 2:11; 17:8), but before Pentecost, they were not believers in a New Testament sense (Jn. 14:12, 29; 16:29–33; 11:11–15, with Mk. 16:17–18).

3. As sons of Israel, they belonged to God (Jn. 17:6), but before Pentecost, they did not have the Spirit within them (Jn. 14:15–17), and so, they were not part of the New Testament "Israel of God" (Rom. 8:9).

4. They loved Jesus (16:27), but before Pentecost, the love of God was not in them (Jn. 17:26) because the Spirit was not in them (cp. Rom. 5:5).

5. They believed that God sent Jesus (Jn. 17:8, 25), but before Pentecost, they did not really know Jesus (Jn. 14:7–9).

6. They were "not of the world" (Jn. 15:18–20; 17:14), but before Pentecost, they were not yet "in Christ" (Jn. 17:21–23, 26). They were like unborn babies (Jn. 16:20–22).

7. They were chosen and ordained (Jn. 15:16), but before Pentecost, they could neither bear to hear all the truth (Jn. 16:12) nor ask the Father anything in Jesus' name (Jn. 16:23–26).

Have you received your personal Pentecost experience? As Paul told young Timothy, "Lay hold on eternal life!" Don't settle for being clean; lay hold on sanctification! Don't settle for believing that God exists and that Jesus came from Him; lay hold on genuine knowledge of God and His Son! Don't settle for reading about Jesus in the Bible; lay hold on fellowship with him in the Spirit! Don't settle for being called or for desiring God's promises. Lay hold on the promise itself, the holy Spirit! The disciples did.

When Is a Person Born Again?

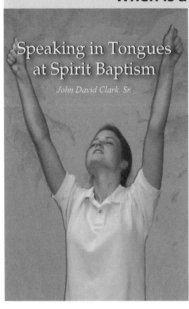

"If any man have not the Spirit of Christ, he is none of his"

We need to know who has received the Spirit of God and who has not. Otherwise, we are lost in a world of religious confusion as to who really is born of God and who is not, which is the condition that exists among believers of today.

This booklet presents an accurate and consistent biblical explanation for speaking in tongues being the "initial evidence" of being baptized with the Spirit.

If true, this belief radically alters the commonly accepted picture of the body of Christ, for since the baptism of the Spirit is the only means of entering the body of Christ (1Cor. 12:13), then the body of Christ is composed only of those who have received that baptism, with the evidence of speaking in tongues. Study *Speaking in Tongues at Spirit Baptism* for straightforward, biblical answers about this important subject.

Where Is Hell? Who Goes There?

Can anyone escape from Hell? Is Hell the "Lake of Fire"?

Our objective in this study was to find out what the Bible really says about the abode of the dead so that we can separate fact from fiction. No tradition, no belief, no opinion was immune from critical examination in the light of what we would find in the Bible.

It seems odd that the study of Hell and the other gruesome places of spiritual damnation could inspire a gentle and deep loving care for others, and yet, that is what we experienced. How could such a thing be? Holy love is perceived generally to be such a tender thing, and, by contrast, Hell is a place where tenderness can only be remembered, never experienced. Nevertheless, this study produced in us a sense of the love and goodness of God that is always directed toward men. In truth, and to our happy surprise, this work proved to be more a story of God than of Hell.

Who Is in Charge of Our Suffering?

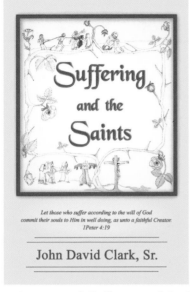

Let those who suffer according to the will of God commit their souls to Him in well doing, as unto a faithful Creator.
1Peter 4:19

John David Clark, Sr.

"And we know that all things work together for good to them that love God, to them who are the called according to His purpose."

You are hurting. You have suffered a crushing loss. You have been disappointed, misunderstood, betrayed. What are you to do? What do you think?

Suffering and the Saints takes you through beautiful Biblical stories of faith where men and women are not only seen doing good in desperate situations but, more than that, the reason they did good is explained. By knowing what they knew, we can do what they did, and be what they were, and receive the strength to continue in well doing.

As you read *Suffering and the Saints*, stand in awe of the goodness, power, and wisdom of God by which the saints of old met and overcame the suffering that God gave them to endure and by which we may also endure our trials and corrections.

Tithes and Offerings

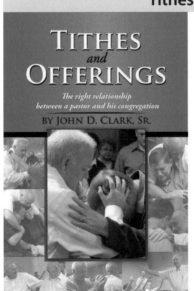

The right relationship between a pastor and his congregation

This is not a book about money. It is a book about the proper relationship of a pastor and his flock, both his responsibility toward them and theirs toward him. How to deal with God's money is a necessary element of the discussion, but the more important issue is, how are we to deal with each other?

Upon reading this manuscript, one lady commented, "Every sentence will be a new thought to God's people." That may not altogether be the case, but many of the sentences in this book certainly will bring new thoughts to those who read them. The truth about tithes and offerings will help to heal the current mass confusion concerning the issue. But be warned; the truth of the matter will challenge your heart with light which, to my knowledge, is shining nowhere else.

Books by John D. Clark, Sr.

Spiritual Light

Suffering and the Saints

The Apostate Fathers

Speaking in Tongues at Spirit Baptism

What Does the Bible Really Say About Hell?

Is the Bible the Word of God?

Marriage and Divorce

Solomon's Wisdom

God Had a Son - *before Mary Did*

Tithes and Offerings

Malachi

—◦◦◦—

For free book downloads or links to order hard copies:

www.GoingtoJesus.com

Final Note from the Author

When we carefully study the disciples' actions and words in the time between Jesus' death and the day of Pentecost, we are forced to look at ourselves and to wonder if we are missing what should be obvious, just as they missed what is now obvious to us. They are us, just living at a different time. May God give us the same grace that He gave to them, that we, too, might escape spiritual blindness and walk with Jesus in the light. If He does that for us, we will rejoice with the apostle who said, "The God who commanded light to shine out of darkness has shone in our hearts to give us the light of the knowledge of the glory of God in the face of Jesus Christ" (2Cor. 4:6).

May God richly bless you!